Then & Now
SALISBURY

This picture of Councillor James Hussey dates from 1843, at the start of his mayoral year, and it is the earliest known photograph of a Salisbury mayor. Councillor Hussey came from a very well known local family and for many years he lived at The Wardrobe in the Cathedral Close, now the Royal Gloucestershire, Berkshire and Wiltshire Regiment Museum. It is quite remarkable that his photograph has survived at all because the positive/negative photographic process had only been introduced three years earlier by William Henry Fox Talbot, of Lacock Abbey in Wiltshire.

Then & Now
SALISBURY

PETER DANIELS & TIM GARRAWAY JONES

TEMPUS

The Market Place in 1956. The names of shops and associated companies to be seen in this photograph are now fading memories in the minds of the older generations, but others have survived and are still providing a valuable service. Let us take a stroll along Ox Row. Pictured from the left: Nos 6,7, Diffeys' Cafeteria and Restaurant; No. 8, Market Inn, selling Gibbs Mew & Company ales; No. 9, E. & G. Crouch, high-class fruiterers and greengrocers; No. 11, City Arms, selling Fussell's ales; No. 12, Mac Fisheries, fishmongers; No. 13, Pearks' Stores, provisions merchant; No. 14a, Farrar's Transport Café; No. 14b, Eastmans Limited, butchers.

First published 2003

Tempus Publishing Limited
The Mill, Brimscombe Port,
Stroud, Gloucestershire, GL5 2QG

British Library Cataloguing in Publication Data.
A catalogue record for this book is available from the British Library.

ISBN 0 7524 3012 2

Typesetting and origination by Tempus Publishing Limited
Printed in Great Britain by Midway Colour Print, Wiltshire

CONTENTS

A rare view of medieval Salisbury – the Old George Hotel yard as it was in 1879. The Old George inn was purchased by Salisbury Council in 1414 and it remained in their ownership for 450 years. The building was sold again in 1863, at which time the licence lapsed. A century later, in 1967, the area around the inn was redeveloped by the Hammerson Group and the Old George Hotel became the High Street entrance to the Old George Mall shopping precinct. The earliest known photograph of the inn dates from 1859, a copy of which is reproduced on p. 56.

INTRODUCTION

Salisbury is a city with a fascinating early history and there is much to be learned about this by studying its old streets and buildings. We owe much of what we know about its recent history to the countless old images that have survived from the past century and a half since the art of photography was born. The images in this book have been selected from the archive of photographs of Wiltshire and the West Country assembled by Peter Daniels over a period of more than twenty-five years, and each old image has been matched with a modern photograph also by Peter Daniels, taken from the same position, allowing the reader to make fascinating comparisons of 'Then & Now'. Sometimes the changes we see are surprisingly small but at other times the two scenes show little in common, so much has changed. All who know and love Salisbury will enjoy seeing it as it was and making the comparisons with the more familiar city of today.

We are most easily reminded of the city's ancient history from the buildings that remain a feature of its landscape, and through these pictures we can see how they have continued to model and shape its growth up to the present day. One of Salisbury's great features is that it was built as a new city, planned and constructed on virgin soil. It developed on rectangular-shaped plots known as chequers. Some buildings, even today, remain within the setting of these original chequers and some of their names live on. An old map by Naish (1751), for example, shows many of these names and the reader will find reference to some of the surviving ones in the course of this book.

As Salisbury grew it spread beyond the boundaries of the old medieval street plan, over neighbouring hillsides and towards the valleys of the five rivers. Outlying villages, like nearby Harnham were eventually embraced by the city's growth. It is interesting to note from the photographs how many changes have occurred to the appearance of even some of the oldest surviving buildings during the last century. See, for example, how the timber-framed premises of St John's Street have undergone subtle alterations during the last century as restoration and modernisation progressed.

One of the best viewpoints from which to get an idea of how the old city was laid out is to climb the 332 steps up the tower of Salisbury Cathedral. There, at Eight Doors level, one can pick out the still prominent landmarks of old buildings in their old chequers and view the street systems of medieval Salisbury. From the base of the spire the visitor can also see Old Sarum, the hill fort where a stone keep once dominated the area before Salisbury was born. One may also look out to the suburbs that swallowed up the clusters of old villages that were once the city's nearest neighbours.

We hope you will enjoy this trail around the streets and environs of Salisbury.

Tim Garraway Jones

The Cathedral Church of the Blessed Virgin Mary as seen from the air in the late 1950s or early 1960s. Salisbury is proud to be home to one of the finest mediaeval cathedrals in Britain, and to many its Close is the loveliest place in England. There is so much to be seen from this high level, and such is the value of a photograph like this that each time it is scrutinised one finds something new - a detail that has not been noticed before. One can be kept entertained for ages. There are many features that have changed since this image was created. Long gone is the Salisbury Council yard that can be seen in the right foreground in an area of The Friary then known as Bugmore. In the distance, beyond the Cathedral spire, an open space comes into view which is now the leisure grounds known as Queen Elizabeth Gardens, developed to commemorate the Coronation of Queen Elizabeth II in 1953. To the right of the pleasure gardens lies the Salisbury General Infirmary, which was vacated relatively recently and redeveloped quite superbly into residential units.

Chapter 1

HARNHAM

This charming scene shows Harnham when it truly was a rural backwater, with thatched buildings in Ayleswade Road. Bishop Bingham's medieval bridge (*c.* 1245) is in the background and some local carters have been caught by the camera as they approached the Swan Inn. The old Swan has now been replaced and other buildings in this scene demolished to make way for modern houses.

The Three Crowns at West Harnham is over 300 years old. The motorist posing here for the photograph is perhaps also the licensee. The car is a two-seater Morris with a dickey seat. It is interesting to see how little this view has changed today. The brick chimney-stack is still standing and the pedestrian bridge and bay window have also survived, but the paper factory seen to the rear of the building has now gone. Gerard John Bates and Roger Jackson, seen in this recent view, became licensees in 1989.

This old view of the mill at Harnham in 1875 is taken from a stereograph. The mill has served many functions, including time as a store for cathedral muniments. A plaque on the wall claims thirteenth-century origins for part of the building's fabric. Timber framing and a doorway at the first-storey level have disappeared by the time of the recent view. Standing outside the front door in the recent view are restaurateurs Malcolm and Deborah ('The Boss') Purvis. A millstone is incorporated into a nearby wall at the property.

A view of the countryside near to Bishop's Walk at West Harnham. The earlier photograph was snapped on VE Day, 1945, with a family gathered outside 4 Kent Road. The recent picture taken at the same spot shows Tim Ayers and his wife Joy (née Middleton) and Tim's daughter Lisa standing with her husband David. The family moved here in 1964, but have now moved to North Devon.

The Swan Inn sold Gibbs Mew ales at the time of this old photograph when Mr Billet was landlord. A sign on the door promotes the sales of Martell's Brandy. It is now The Greyfisher Inn. The old building has survived well and the chimneys and stone mullions are all still in place. The original porch has been enclosed; other buildings have been extended, and the first-floor doorway into the coachhouse has been removed. The Greyfisher continued to sell Gibbs Mew ales until the brewery was sold off in the closing years of the twentieth century. These beers which are now produced by Ushers were delivered by shire horse and cart until quite recently and even the Bishop of Salisbury received his regular quota of 'Bishop's Tipple' by this means.

De Vaux Place was the site of Salisbury's first place of learning and fragments of the old – and now lost – De Vaux College may still be found incorporated into the old walls. The substantial houses here have undergone much restoration and refurbishment and they stand adjacent to a busy corner of the old city, Harnham Gate, the southerly entrance into the Cathedral Close. The old postcard view shows local residents on bicycles and pushing a pram; there is a handcart in the foreground. The wrought iron gates have gone but an extra Victorian-style lamp has now been erected. At the time of the earlier photograph C.J. Rattue, who lived at the Bridle Path in the Close, had the responsibility of lighting the gas lamps in the Cathedral Close for the Dean and Chapter.

In 1897, the date of this old photograph, 'Diamond' Joe Curtis was the boot and shoemaker, occupying a site between the Swan Inn and Ayleswade Bridge. It is interesting to note that Harnham possessed its own street lighting at this time. Mr Curtis probably did very well in this location as visitors to the city entering from the south all crossed the old bridge and in so doing passed his front door. The adjacent buildings, although looking a little 'tumbledown', are reasonably intact and could perhaps have been preserved. They have, however, perished and eventually made way for number 13 Ayleswade Road, now home of the Robert's family.

This terrace of thatched cottages in Old Street, Harnham belonged to Mr Russ in 1964. They appear to have been simple 'two-up and two-down' houses with shuttered windows downstairs. The thatched house at the end of the street has been replaced by garages and the adjacent flint house has also gone. However, although these buildings disappeared as a result of slum clearance, to be replaced by a brick-built terrace, a neighbouring row of old cottages still stands, just up the road from the Rose and Crown Hotel. They give us an idea of what the other cottages in Old Street might have looked like.

These detached, thatched cottages were also located quite near to the Rose and Crown Hotel, giving the impression that East Harnham was a small community of old cottages. The nearest house seems to have been built from stone, chalk and flint but has now been replaced with a brick-built house. The terrace on the left has survived and still looks much the same today. The group of children posing for the photographer may well have been deliberately gathered for the picture but are probably residents of the street.

entrance with stone-capped columns and decorated wrought iron railings; visitors passed through this formal entrance to enjoy a walk or picnic by the river. What is apparently a municipal street lamp is positioned in front of the gates and behind the people is a building, possibly a boathouse, or even the hut that survives near the river to this day. A stone plaque records that the Walk was opened to the public in June 1913 by the generosity of Cllr William Pritchard when mayor (1911-1912). The Exeter Street roundabout now lies over or near to the earlier scene but access to the Riverside Walk, now known as Churchill Gardens, is still enjoyed by folk today. The entrances now include underpasses and the path near St Nicholas Hospital, to the right of both photographs.

This Edwardian view of Riverside Walk comes from a postcard bearing a halfpenny stamp sent to a Woking address in 1913. The location is the end of Exeter Street (once known as Draghall Street) where the busy roundabout now joins up with the city ring road. The photograph shows a brick-built

The Victorian workhouse, Tower House, was off Coombe Road. It was a place that the elderly and infirm greatly feared and did their best to avoid. The Victorian workhouse system was notorious for its harsh treatment of those who became destitute. Tower House was demolished sometime around 1980 and only the chapel, a listed building, survives and remains in use today. The writer can remember inspecting the site, and admiring some flowering japonica's in the neglected gardens there in 1976. Today the housing estate known as Riding's Mead has mushroomed across the hillside and a roundabout has diverted traffic away from the ambulance station in Newbridge Road.

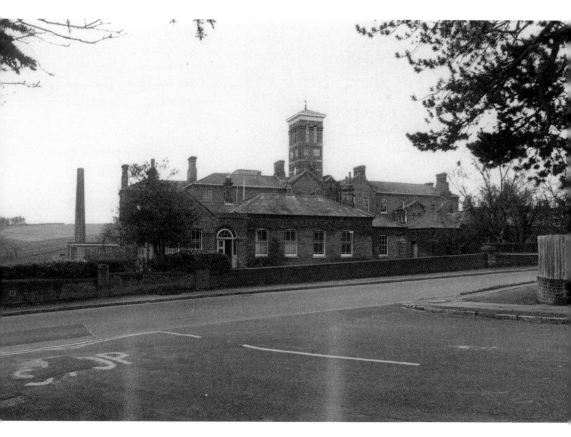

East Harnham taken from an old carte-de-visite photograph. This picture shows the scene looking from New Harnham Road towards the Rose and Crown Hotel, *c.* 1879. The buildings with the chequerboard walls and the adjacent houses have long since vanished, but the terraced houses to the right with the chimney stack have survived. Also visible is a thatched house in Old Street, which is also featured on page 17 of this book. The grassy bank now supports bushes and trees, and a newer house has replaced the thatched one that once stood in this quiet old village of East Harnham.

Children and teachers often seem to look very serious in school photographs from the Victorian period. Possibly this was to do with stricter regimes at school or perhaps simply that they were much less familiar with the camera than children are today. This postcard picture of Class Two at East Harnham School is undated but was sent to Mrs Harris at Bishopstone Rectory as a Christmas card in around 1910. East Harnham School is now a residence next to the church and features on the OS map of 1887. The contemporary picture shows a group of children photographed in the school grounds at Harnham Junior School in Saxon Road, with the headteacher, Jackie Lane, who had been in position at the school from 1997 to 2002, when she retired.

This view of Harnham watermeadows and the cathedral was taken from Bishops Walk in the 1890s. There were fields then between All Saints Church at East Harnham and Parsonage Farm at West Harnham. It was the building of substantial houses like these that began the eventual joining up of the two villages. Today, from left to right, Harnham Croft, Hazelmere and Grasmere occupy these sites and the grounds no longer contain the substantial vegetable plots and orchards of yesteryear.

This picture of two Victorian gentleman in Middle Street was taken by F. Treble in around 1865 as a stereograph. A tributary of the River Nadder flows on the right. Some structural alterations have been made to the Mill House and the building in the new photograph is now known as Old Mill Cottage. Pushing her pram by the Mill House is Linda Baker with baby Jonathan.

West Harnham School for Boys and Girls was less exposed to the road in the early decades of the twentieth century than the building is today. Now it occupies a prominent position at a busy junction and has been used for many years by the Nadder Wines company. Children were transferred to Harnham Primary School on the new site in Saxon Road when this school closed. The old school appears on the OS map of 1887. Just across the road is the historic old Parsonage Farm, a building of such interest that it is listed as an ancient monument.

Winchester Street where it joins Brown Street and Rollestone Street. This photograph from around 1910 clearly shows the angular layout of the streets of Salisbury, or New Sarum as it was originally known. *The Salisbury Guide*, of 1848, sufficiently explains the regular intersection of the streets: 'Bishop Poore divided the ground of the new city into *places,* or chequers as they were commonly known, each measuring seven perches in length and three in width (one perch is equal to 5 ½ yards or 5.029 metres). For each place of such dimensions twelve-pence was paid yearly to the Bishop, six-pence at Easter and six-pence at Michaelmas (29 September)'. The name Davis seems to have dominated this part of Winchester Street in the early 1900s: On the left, at the far corner of Rollestone Street, stands Ralph Davis's general furniture stores and on the extreme right, nearest to the

camera, can be seen Davis's Antique Furniture Warehouse. The Cash Fruit and Flower Stores occupies the shop on the near corner of Brown Street, where one could also go to 'hire horses and carriages'. G. Davis was the proprietor.

Chapter 2

THE OLD CHEQUERS AND THE CITY CENTRE

Austin Underwood took this Box Brownie photograph of the Co-operative furnishing store in 1937 following a disastrous fire on Monday 13 September. The photograph records several architectural features of this now lost building, such as decorated roof gables, shaped-tile cladding and carved wooden timbers above the entrance. A note on the back of the photograph records Underwood's concern at Salisbury's loss; he typed the following: 'Traces of Medieval Salisbury still waited to be demolished on the corner of Milford Street.' The photograph also records that the A36 took the Southampton traffic right through the heart of the city. The new Co-op, now QS, stood on the corner of the Cross Keys chequer, with just a token architectural feature above the entrance of an otherwise plain modern building.

How many hostelries have stood on the site of the White Horse Hotel, the building which shares its name with this historic chequer off Castle Street? The earlier building here seems grand enough and yet it appears to have been replaced by the current building. Look carefully at both pictures though, for it may be that there was not a complete replacement but rather an alteration or 'facelift'. The arrangement of some windows and the positioning of the entrance are the same but the shape of the front is otherwise quite radically changed. The stone quoins to the right-hand side suggest that the building next door has not changed.

Roy Grace (left) stands outside the inn with Keith Marcham and Scott and Kim Dodge from Warminster.

Castle Street. Salisbury.

The premises belonging to George Breeze, newsagent and postcard seller, at 9 Castle Street stood opposite the Blew Bore chequer, but it seems that the downstairs shop has now been incorporated into today's Tesco building. Only the upstairs second and third storeys seem to have survived to the present day. The rest of Mr Breeze's neighbours' shops have been swept away. This old postcard was sent to a Liverpool address in 1914.

The Catherine Wheel at 33 Milford Street was a 'tied house' owned and managed by Blandford brewers Hall & Woodhouse. At the time of this photograph, 1929, Chas. Wm. Noble managed the pub and his neighbours were W. Goddard & Co. at No. 35, Sparks & Yeates at No. 31 and Wm. Sewell (furnisher) at No. 29. These buildings all stood in Black Horse chequer. More recently the inn became the Trafalgar Hotel, perhaps because of a local connection with Lord Nelson. Nelson's family inherited a local house after his death at the Battle of Trafalgar in 1805. The front of the building, at least, has seen some major alterations. The ladies' hairdressing salon next door has also seen changes. A sign announces that umbrellas can be repaired and recovered - one wonders how much custom for this there would be today. Billboards outside the Catherine Wheel make interesting reading: *The Sport of Kings*, 'a sparkling comedy' presented by the Porton Experimental Station Dramatic Society, and *Guns of Loos*, a 'stupendous attraction' starring Henry Victor and Hermione Baddeley.

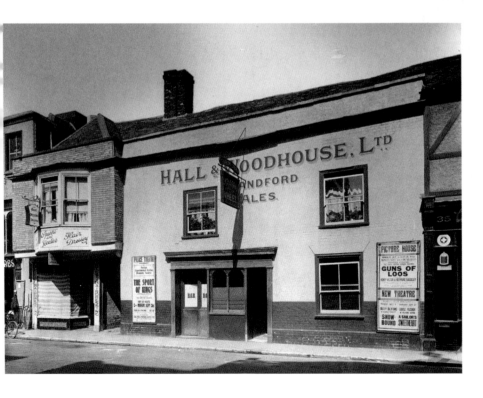

which enjoy views of the cathedral spire. Different uses for this one-time merchant's residence have included a lodging house, antiques shop and art gallery, although it was originally built for cathedral use and was once known as The Cloisters. The modern photograph depicts Mr and Mrs Irvin St George at the door of their home.

Jessie Browning, bootmaker and repairer, traded from 3 St John Street, in White Hart chequer. The early picture of the premises was taken sometime after 1906. Next door on the right was James Marsh, fruiterer, with Thomas Sanger, blacksmith, to the left. This old building, reputedly built in the fifteenth century, has been beautifully restored, revealing the timber framing and keeping all the windows. It is part of a jettied hall house which was built partly from timber salvaged from shipping. There are now three windows in the roof

Silver Street with Leaver's shop – basket, sieve and chairmaker – just across the way from the Poultry Cross. It is pictured in the 1880s, but according to directories had gone by 1897. The older building, the Salisbury Supply, has been well preserved but the other buildings have been replaced.

Salisbury High Street, with the NAAFI Club decorated for the Queen's Coronation in 1953. It stood opposite the New Street chequer, and is a site now more familiarly occupied by a Woolworths store. A Morris motor car is parked at the front entrance; this would certainly not be possible for any car to do today as the street is pedestrianised. This photograph was provided by Mrs C. Walker who worked with the WVS at the NAAFI club.

Austin Underwood captured a feeling of the seventies with this view of Gigant Street and the framework of the bridge for the infamous plan that would also have cut a new road across Catherine Street. Austin noted on the back of his photograph that: 'only a fiercely-fought local public inquiry and public opinion defeated the aims of this structure… which would have been a Bridge Too Far'. Just in view on the left of this picture are the buildings of Gibbs Mew Brewery and the Anchor Inn. Gigant Street has recently seen substantial redevelopment, and the brewery has closed and been sold. Gibbs Mew Ales were brewed under licence by Ushers of Trowbridge for a while but this brewery has recently ceased to brew and has also closed. Gigant Street is situated between Rolfe's chequer and Trinity chequer.

This 1860s view shows the Market House, along with other buildings on the old Blew Bore chequer, now Blue Boar Row. The Market House was officially opened on 24 May 1859 and was linked to the national railway network with its own line. The railway bridge may still be seen at the rear of the library which now occupies this building. The market building was designed by Mr Strapp of the South Western Railway who specified that Bath stone was to be used for this handsome classical façade. The building has also been known as the Corn Exchange. Today's view demonstrates just how things have changed – gone is the open expanse of the Market Place which is now filled with cars, trees and modern street furniture. There have been many changes to the façade of Blue Boar Row but the Market House front has hardly altered at all.

According to the date on this postcard view of Blue Boar Row, it shows a scene in 1838. This is not possible, as photography was still to be invented at that time, but it is certainly from the late nineteenth century. The postcard was sold by R.R. Edwards Ltd of Castle Street. The Saracen's Head Inn has long since disappeared and other buildings have acquired new fronts and been expanded. Only the building now used by Lloyds Pharmacy bears a striking resemblance to the original.

In the New Street chequer, now known as New Canal, once stood the Salisbury and Wiltshire Library building with, at the time of the photograph, the shop belonging to James Gater. The flags suggest a celebration, perhaps the Coronation of Edward VII in 1902. The building has survived well, at least on the upper floors, and Gater's shop has been replaced by the Cargo Home Shop. It is interesting to compare the styles of dress worn by the two youths in the photographs, separated by a century of change.

This jettied, timber–framed house at 88 Milford Street (St Martin's Club at the time of the photograph) originated in the fifteenth century and was dismantled in 1972 to be removed to Lockeridge near Marlborough for a rebuild project. It was probably originally part of a larger medieval hall house. William Marchy, tailor, owned a tenement here in 1479, situated on the northern side of the Barnard's Cross chequer. The building was removed to make way for the ring road development and in particular the road bridge across Milford Street at its junction with Rampart Road.

This is Queen Street in 1945. The house directly behind the uniformed police sergeant is William Russell's House (No. 9) dating from 1306. William Russell was a wool merchant and his original house would have been a medieval hall, open inside without an upstairs but with a sleeping platform and perhaps a hole in the roof for the smoke to escape. Familiar names that have occupied the premises across the centuries include Harding, Ray, Marshman and Hussey (all clothiers or weavers); Creeds (basketmakers) and the Fort family (hatters) from Alderbury House. At the time of this photograph Mence Smith sold household items. Watson & Co. originally began to sell china and glass in 1834 from Ye Halle of John Halle in New Canal, transferring to No. 8 Queen Street, The House of John A'Port, next door, in 1930. This house was built in 1425 by a merchant prince of that name; he was six times Mayor of Salisbury. It occupied land on the old Three Lion chequer.

Members of the Volunteer Fire Brigade, whose engine was called *The Alert*, photographed in 1911 at the time of George V's coronation, and their modern equivelants today taking centre stage for a photograph before the Guildhall. The Wiltshire Fire Brigade, photographed in 2001, included sub-officer Peter Covington-Jones and fire-fighters Byron Standen, Paul Noke, Ben Haughian and Nick Barrett. The earlier photograph includes the statue of Sydney Herbert, Minister for War during the Crimean conflict and friend of Florence Nightingale, since removed to Victoria Park.

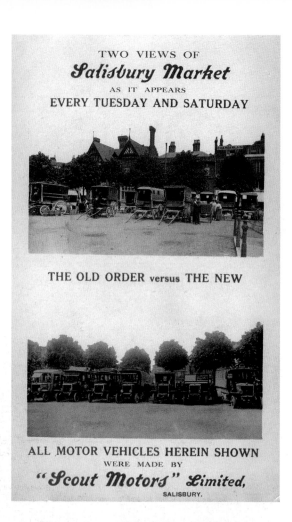

TWO VIEWS OF

Salisbury Market

AS IT APPEARS

EVERY TUESDAY AND SATURDAY

THE OLD ORDER versus THE NEW

ALL MOTOR VEHICLES HEREIN SHOWN

WERE MADE BY

"*Scout Motors*" *Limited*,

SALISBURY.

This picture postcard from 1914 features its own 'Then and Now' comparison of old and new vehicles by the Guildhall in the Market Place. This historic view of carriers carts and wagons, and Scout Motor vehicles, belongs to yesteryear, for these vehicles have now all disappeared down Memory Lane. Scout Motors was a Salisbury firm founded in 1902 and closed down in 1921. The trees are a feature of all the pictures; as in many city centres, they are plane trees and lime trees, both species happy to tolerate the pollution found in cities.

The Corn Exchange played host to the Golden Jubilee Trades Exhibition in 1962. Today the City Library remains the focus of much activity for book-lovers of all ages. It is interesting to see that a contemporary clock has been inserted into the classical façade of the historic building and that the place name Cornmarket survives in the adjacent inn. Market Walk now leads across the River Avon where trains once carried corn to the local branch line.

In 1945 busy Blue Boar Row was dominated by the imposing store of Style & Gerrish (now Debenhams) along with the Cadena Café and the WVS. As for the motorist, there are few opportunities now for driving that way towards the Cornmarket - it is one-way traffic only! The driver of the Ford Popular may have been a visitor, as the number plate ALK732 was registered in London sometime after 1933. Traffic-calming measures have also recently come into place as part of the district council's policy towards making the city centre a safer and more pleasant place for the visitor.

A corn and seed merchant traded in an historically appropriate context on the corner of Oatmeal Row, but now the Portman Building Society occupies this busy corner of the Market Place. The markets are a feature as old as the cathedral itself and were recognised by 1361. Bull's book stall, open to the elements here in around 1930, attracted the interest of passers-by. A modern weather-proof stall with garden ornaments occupies the same spot today during market days

A Recruiting Office banner dominates Minster Street, recruiting for the First World War. There is a wealth of interesting detail in this view; some of the traders to be spotted include Lipton's, later to be Boots, to the right, along with other famous companies such as Halfords, Stead & Simpson and Macey & Jefferey, tobacconists. Stead & Simpson are still to be found at No. 17, but are now known as Footwear Retailers. An island safe-haven has been installed today at this busy junction, complete with bollards, traffic lights and pedestrian crossings.

Staff line up for the camera at the International Stores in Oatmeal Row in around 1910. Here you could buy choice teas, finest quality meats and a variety of tinned and bottled produce, seen here stacked up in the window. Only the old metal drain pipes in the photograph reveal that this is one and the same building, presently occupied by Portman Building Society. Some decorative stonework survives too but is not visible in the old photograph.

In 1932, at Lipton's in Silver Street, twelve staff posed for the firm's picture at a time when seven old pence bought a pound of cocoa powder. On special offer was Rangoon Rice: three pounds for ten pence. Notice the hanging hams and bacons, and the eggs and meats in the window. Was this obedient dog the firm's mascot? Pictured outside Boots in the modern photograph is the branch manager, Phillip Woods, and members of his staff.

The Boots logo has hardly changed over the years although the Salisbury store has moved around the city a bit. By 1931 it occupied this site in the High Street but had also traded from 29–31 Fisherton Street. Bingham & Sons were to be found here before Boots. The building hardly seems to have changed, but the entrance has shifted away from the corner. In the old view the shop formerly occupied by MacFisheries can be seen. From these shops today one can purchase clothing, artwork, book an exotic holiday or eat a burger. Old timber framing has been revealed during restorations to the building used by Lunn Poly.

The International Stores, with a staff of ten, was to be found at 18 High Street in 1922 when, as now, margarine was cheaper to buy. However, perishable provisions are not to be found these days in the High Street and today the premises are occupied by an educational toys company. Perhaps only the number twenty survives as a clue to where we are. Posing for the modern view are Sylvia Fower (acting manager) with Christine Moore (left) and Clare McNeill. The shop opened in December 1986.

Before the International Stores was to be found at Oatmeal Row, Salisbury family firm Main & Sons were the corn and seed merchants trading from New Sarum House at the site. They had a mill in Fisherton Street, now the art and craft gallery where visitors can stroll round and still find antiquated machinery associated with the corn milling trade. This old squat building was demolished to make way for the more prosperous-looking Victorian establishment now inhabited by the Portman Building Society.

Woolworths in Silver Street was decorated for the Silver Jubilee of George V in 1935. The firm was once proud to state that they sold nothing over sixpence and perhaps as a result of that policy they quickly outgrew their premises and had to find a larger store. That was to be the old NAAFI club around the corner in the High Street, as we have seen earlier. The same site in Silver Street today provides a variety of services and goods, but the splendidly symmetrical shopfront of past times has now gone.

A commemorative arch in St Ann Street to mark the Coronation of Edward VII in 1902 provides a view looking east towards Barnards Cross chequer on the left. Two boys pose like sentries by the arch which stood outside what is now The Bakers Arms at 32 St Ann Street. Margaret Turner sold jewellery from her workshop here at No. 15. An almshouse once stood in this street and Friar's Bridge once crossed a watercourse at the junction with Brown Street. The whole of St Ann Street is filled with architecture spanning several centuries and one can just imagine the bustle of this once busy corner of Salisbury, filled with the tradesmen who provided the lifeblood of the city.

centre of the picture, that hardly seems to have changed externally at all, once looked out over Friar's Bridge. The water now travels under the ground here. It once fed the paper mills near Bugmore (now the Friary), before returning to the Avon at today's Churchill Gardens.

Looking west in St Ann Street on a warm and sunny September day in 1926, three girls wearing hats caught the photographer's eye. Many of the buildings here have survived well. On the left is the St Ann Joinery Works providing a reminder that this plot of medieval Salisbury provided carpenters for the building of the cathedral. The Joiners Hall in St Ann Street dates from the early seventeenth century and can be found at Nos 56–58. Next to the Joinery Works stood another trade's premises, now gone to make way for the entrance to Green Court. The timber-framed house in the

The Ox Row Inn in the Market Place, later the City Arms Inn, a licensed public house here advertising Old Irish Whiskey. Upstairs, Hilliard & Younge had a saloon with a good view from the bay window of the busy market that traditionally took place on Saturdays and Tuesdays. Markets had a distinctive agricultural character in past times. The popular Ox Row Inn now has a more modern appearance after the passing of ninety years. The new manager is Nicola Shearing and she has a staff of eight to help prepare and serve food as well as drink, seven days a week.

The High Street in the early twentieth century housed considerably more businesses than it does today. In 1908 thirty-five different trades were managed by forty-eight companies. This postcard was sent to a London address in 1937. Familiar names of city trades visible here include Suttons, the Old George Hotel, Boyes on the left, Brinsmeads Music Stores, Tovey, Miriam Gray and the Crown Hotel on the right – names which may jog a few memories. Frederick Sutton ran his tobacco, confectionery and restaurant business at 11–13 High Street and employed a Swiss chef. Today the High Street looks very different with its traffic-free, pedestrianised pavements.

The North Gate in the High Street photographed in the 1860s, with the former Porter's Lodge (No. 48) and the College of Matron's Almshouse, built in around 1682, both visible behind the archway. What is now the SPCK bookshop was then David Newman's shoe shop and next door to that was John Brittan's shop. The North Gate dates from the fourteenth century and the wall incorporates carved stonework thought to have come from Old Sarum. In the fifteenth century a portcullis was added and this was controlled from the guardroom above. The grooves used by the portcullis are still visible. The royal coat of arms belongs to the Stuarts, perhaps commemorating the restoration of the monarchy in the seventeenth century.

The George Inn, High Street, around 1859. The inn looks its age in this old view and even then it was part of a building of four to five hundred years of age. This impressive hostelry, which has given its name to the modern shopping mall behind, had a long tradition of innkeeping, but was also used at one stage as a dwelling house. The George was a popular focus for Victorian artists, and many good views survive to show what the inn once looked like. The picture also shows the shop belonging to John Humby, baker and pastrycook, and that of George Sydenham, boot and shoe manufacturer. Further down the road can be seen the Assembly Rooms, now Waterstones Bookshop, which once had a more elaborate façade and porch.

A very early view of the Poultry Cross, before 1852. The Cross dates from about 1450 and is roughly the same age as the nearby Haunch of Venison inn. The Victorians added a 'crown' to this late-medieval structure during the 1850s, making a dramatic alteration to its appearance. The old photograph also shows how the timber framing on the buildings behind the cross was covered up with rendering at that time. Family jewellers W. Carter & Sons have not moved far from this site and the general street scene has not altered much either over a century and a half. Baker and confectioner 'Vivean' is long gone from the building on the right, which probably also has jettied, timber framing preserved under its hanging tiles.

There have always been some familiar names trading from this ancient corner of the city. Here at the corners of Silver Street and Minster Street in the 1960s there are four in a row! Marks & Spencer have since moved to the New Street chequer and although it seems a long time since Timothy Whites or Lipton's were trading in Salisbury, Olivers shoes have remained in place beyond the millennium. Meanwhile, the Haunch of Venison across the road has a name that has transcended several centuries.

New Canal has long been a place to park vehicles. The traps parked underneath the trees here create a picturesque scene. Two buildings are of particular interest in this scene. One is the hostelry (advertising Dorchester Ales & Stout) that must surely be an Eldridge & Pope inn, and that nowadays houses the Bradford & Bingley Building Society. Underneath today's hairdressing saloon will be the cellars used by former businesses here, and the flagpole above these premises in the earlier picture suggests it may have had a more significant, perhaps civic, role in those distant days.

New Canal full of cars and buses on a wet day in the early 1950s. The photograph is a source of historical information because it shows several buildings which were demolished in 1967. In fact, these three-storey brick-built shopfronts were eighteenth-century facades which were added to older buildings already present. The older buildings were remodelled to make more efficient use of the restricted space available.

Edward Naish's Garage was situated at the west end of New Street (north side), at Nos 70–74. The name Naish is listed in Kelly's Directory under the heading 'Commercial', and it appears from 1925 to 1941/42. At some stage the garage seems to have been bought up by Edwards Brothers Motor Engineers, who also traded from New Street at Nos 54–58. They also had workshops in Friary Lane, with premises in High Street in 1912 and the 'Canal', and by 1950 they had become the main Ford dealers. Edward J. Naish, Motor Engineer, may have known his colleagues well; perhaps that is him in the photograph admiring the vehicle with its proud owner? Modern buildings have now been constructed at this site. The Old George Shopping Mall lies to the rear of these buildings.

Old houses in Chipper Lane next to the old post office in 1929. The General Post Office is on the extreme left and the next two houses were for a great number of years the offices of Messrs Lee, Houseman & Powning, solicitors; later the firm was known as Powning, Jones & Parker. Mr Lee and Mr Powning were at different periods town clerks of the city. These premises were eventually bought by the Post Office for future extensions. The house next to the solicitors was occupied by 'George Holt, carriage proprietor'. The Salisbury Library was also housed in Chipper Lane before relocating to the Corn Exchange.

Dr Gilbert Kemp MD lived at 17 Endless Street, at the junction with Chipper Lane. He was listed under 'Surgeons' in the 1912 edition of Kelly's Directory. At that time, the letterbox in the street was cleared nine times daily! By 1930, a Chas. Gilbert B. Kempe, MD, OBE, MRCS, at the same address was described as Physician and Surgeon. He was a Licentiate of the Royal College of Physicians of London. Local tailor, Mr Hurford, remembered a relative receiving an operation from Mr Kempe at the premises. Entertainment followed medical practice with the building of the Regal Cinema in 1937, part of Associated British Cinemas Ltd.

Sewell's Furnishing Stores at 21 Milford Street was photographed in the late nineteenth century, possibly as early as 1880. The wares were spread out across three bays of shopfront and customers were able to choose their bathtubs, buckets or pans before even setting foot in the shop. Nowadays, some of those items are more likely to contain summer plants in courtyard gardens. It is interesting to see that the property is today split into two businesses. The old sash windows have survived in one building. The roof lines suggest that an old building with fine timbers lurks within, and records show that this roof is in fact a rare survivor from part of a medieval tenement house known as The Bolehall, which was in the hands of Philip Aubyn in 1319 and is therefore one of the city's oldest residential fragments.

Endless Street as it appeared on a postcard mailed to Kidderminster in 1908. The Palace (late County Hall) stood opposite Dr Kempe's house (see page 63) on the corner at 15 Endless Street. In Kelly's Directory (1912) it was described thus:

a fine imposing building in the style of Queen Anne, erected in 1889 by its proprietor, Mr Arthur Whitehead. The building seats 1,240 persons comfortably and has exceptionally appointed stage exits going outwards to render it an extremely safe building in case of fire.

Another list in the Directory for No. 15 mentions Salisbury Municipal offices and W.J. Goodwin, Corporation Surveyor; F. Hodding, Town Clerk; and Albany Ward's

Electric Variety Palace. By 1950 an entry in the Directory mentioned the Palace Garage (English's) Ltd, Motor Engineers, along with the County Police Station. Today, The master Locksmith is a familiar landmark on the corner.

This view looks down Catherine Street from the junction with New Street in 1937 and is from a postcard produced by the Fisherton Street photographers, Futcher & Son. The whole of the street, including the forecourt of Wessex Motors, is festooned with decorations to celebrate the Coronation of George VI. Wessex Motors Ltd already had premises in Southampton Road in 1925, and in 1950 were to be found on the corner at 6 New Street and 60 Catherine Street. They could be telephoned on two numbers at that time, 3275 and 3276. They traded as motor car distributors and engineers, with garages and petrol service stations. Wessex Motors Ltd were also to be found at Wilton Road in Salisbury. For many years the building which replaced the garage was used by the insurance company Friend's Provident until they outgrew their offices.

ilford Street from a postcard dated 1910. The coal merchant undled his load into town towards a ustling street filled with activity. Vhere groceries were once sold, rpets are now the significant item at e corner of Culver Street. Opposite, n the corner of Guilder Lane, a fteenth-century timbered house that oked distinctly neglected in 1910 d is seen here with closed shutters its windows, has today acquired big odern windows and lost the ndering that obscured its timber ame.

Plume of Feathers Yard, as it was in 1898. Considering its great age and location, it is quite remarkable that these ancient steps have survived. Constructed in the seventeenth century, the picturesque staircase is now a familiar feature in the Cross Keys Shopping Centre. The Plume of Feathers inn was undoubtedly a popular place in the seventeenth and eighteenth centuries – a report from the year 1752 announced that 'the Plume of Feathers in Market Place is now completely fitted up and made commodious'.

Chapter 3

WEST OF THE CITY CENTRE

Salisbury station in the 1945, with several people in military uniform, as a Southern Railway, Maunsell-designed, Class N15 or King Arthur express passenger 4-6-0, pulls into the platform. This 1925-built locomotive, *Sir Menadeuke,* was later renumbered by British Railways. There is little change in the appearance of this platform today.

shopping centre known as The Maltings. The picture reveals just how extensive an operation the malting process was, with large warehouses utilised for the purpose. Barley was steeped in water until it began to sprout and was then roasted in kilns. The Bishop's Mill has survived along with the old control hatches to give a flavour of times past. Now a public house, it featured as the 'Town Mill' on William Naish's map of 1751. The central car park created by the developments from wasteland provides extensive car parking for modern Salisbury's visitors and shoppers. The Maltings buildings are nowadays dominated by Sainsbury's supermarket.

Many people will remember the malthouses seen in this picture from 1963. The site was in a state of dereliction for many years before being developed into the current

The Royal Exchange Assurance building in Bridge Street bears the date 1720 on the wall. Now, BBC Radio Wiltshire has its local office on the premises and Bateman's opticians have moved slightly to one side, while family jewellers H.R. Tribbeck & Son are still in place at the end of the block. The tower of St Thomas's Church peeps out over the rooftops.

The Fisherton clock tower has been a familiar landmark on the western approach to the city centre for many years. The earlier photograph is taken from a postcard view from around the turn of the twentieth century and shows the clock tower associated with its long-time partner, the cab drivers' shelter. The cabbies' bothy has gone but a shelter for bus passengers has replaced it. A room at the base of the tower was once used as a lock-up and the stone carving of the prisoners' manacles (taken from a former goal) may still be viewed on the exterior wall. There are also niches in the walls that may once have held statues. The tower is opened for public viewing on rare occasions.

The Maundrel Hall stands opposite the clock tower in Fisherton Street. The general structure of the building appears to have survived to the present day, although with some modifications and modernisations to convert it into its present role as a pub. There was a date mark of 1880 on the front wall that is visible in the earlier view. The building was built as a memorial to a Protestant, John Maundrel, who was burnt at the stake in Fisherton on 24 March 1556. The hall was initially used for evangelistic religious services. During the Second World War it was used as a services club. The old bridge has undergone a few transformations too, with the loss of iron fencing, heraldic shield and gas lamp.

The patriotic efforts of Osmonds, bakers, confectioners and refreshment rooms, are recorded in this photograph of their shop decorated for the Coronation of Edward VII in 1902. The shop was at No. 65 Fisherton Street, where Teed Tools now trade, and next door to Yorkshire Fisheries. The building has not changed fundamentally. As in so many cases of re-use all the alterations are at ground level.

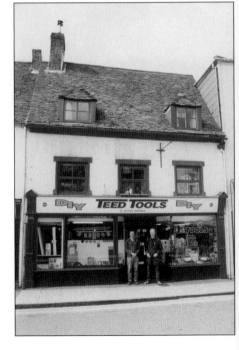

Sarah Hayter's almshouses stood a little way off from the railway bridge, near to the west end of Fisherton Street. Built in the eighteenth century by endowment, they were demolished in 1964, rebuilt, and then rebuilt again around the millennium. Once there were six two-storied dwellings on this site, with a plaque on which was inscribed the following: 'This Asylum built and endow'd for 6 poor women by Mrs Sarah Hayter, lady of this manor, 1797'. The almshouses were one of many established for the city's poor folk, some dating from the seventeenth and eighteenth centuries. Notice the stone quoins which have been included in the new brick-built houses to give the almshouses a distinctive appearance, contrasting with the very simple construction of the original building.

The junction of St Paul's Road and Wilton Road seen in the earlier photograph in the 1960s. Many houses and St Paul's Primary School were demolished to make way for the new ring road and the roundabout that now dominates this busy site. Henley's Garage on the corner served Shell petrol to passing motorists beneath an elegant little art deco-style clock tower, now sadly missing. Although the garage continued as a petrol station until recent years, it now sits empty and fenced off awaiting decisions about further developments for this area. Norman Lake recorded the 1960s view.

The Fisherton tollgate and tollhouse at St Paul's was relocated to Stratford Road, long before it was thought necessary to build a ring road, with a roundabout by St Paul's Church. It was sold by auction in 1858 and demolished during the 1860s. It was then rebuilt and it is currently used by Avon Lodge Veterinary Service. The almshouses still survive next to the church, catering for the city's elderly and needy, but now at a very much noisier and busier location than of old.

On the northwest route out of the city centre by the Devizes Road stood the Nestlé's factory in Russell Road. This provided labour for a century or more for many of the people who lived in the nearby terraces of two-up and two-downs in the area. By the 1960s it had ceased the processing of milk products and coffee but was still used by Nestlé's for the packing of food products. The factory was demolished in the 1970s and has now been replaced by modern town housing.

This view of St Paul's Road, taken in the early years of the twentieth century, reminds us of how much was changed in this area through the 1960s construction of the ring road. Several roads were cut in half, including George Street and Meadow Road; and St Paul's School, just visible on the right at the end of this view, was lost along with all the houses on the same side of the road. St Paul's Primary School is now located in Westminster Road.

A splendidly evocative view of Cann's Wilton Road Service Station photographed in the 1930s. The garage is now long gone and has been replaced by a bungalow with bed and breakfast facilities in the loft extension. The garage offered four fuels of the period: Pratts gasoline, Power, Shell and National Benzole. You could have booked a bus trip to Bournemouth here too, for Cann was also an agent for the Wilts & Dorset bus company – the board on the forecourt offers trips at 9.30 a.m. and 2.30 p.m. daily for two shillings and sixpence.

The Malmesbury Arms in Wilton Road is seen here decorated for Queen Victoria's Diamond Jubilee in 1897. Jubilees and coronations appear to have created good business for the local photographer. Many pictures taken during such celebrations survive today, commissioned by the publicans and shopkeepers from the local photographer, in this case Mr Rewse of Fisherton Street, to record the occasion and their own efforts to produce the best-dressed building. Mr Harry Parsons was the licensee and one assumes that he is among this group of staff, family members and customers. The house next door was at some stage absorbed into the business and forms part of the present day Hogs Head pub, seen here with the current landlord and customers. At the time of the earlier photograph, No. 1 Malmesbury Cottages, next door, was occupied by Edwin Day, gardener, and his wife Anna, and at No. 2 was Frederick Willis, engine driver.

The Half-Way House Hotel in Wilton Road survives to this day but is now called Tom Brown's, selling Famous Ales. The travellers passing down Wilton Road here in 1907 were probably returning from a day at the races. Carriages were sometimes pestered by 'whippersnappers' – see the boy here trying to get a ride by holding onto the rear of the carriage. Passengers would warn drivers of a 'whip behind', as this practise could be dangerous. Perhaps the modern 'whippersnapper' is the skate-boarding enthusiast who holds onto the rear of a bus in a busy city street today. Nearby Bemerton Heath had not been developed at this time and there was much open countryside near the Wilton Road.

Chapter 4

CASTLE STREET AND NORTH OF THE CITY

Woodrows the ironmongers in Castle Street was much missed when they closed this shop and Tesco opened their first supermarket in part of the same building. There were big changes made at ground level but the frontage above has stayed much the same. In this 1930s photograph of Castle Street the Woodrows vehicle turning into the shop's yard is a Morris Commercial van. Woodrows firm relocated to the Churchfields Industrial Estate in the early 1970s, from where they still trade. The company was founded in 1842.

The Castle Garage in Castle Street, seen around 1930, has, like so many small motor businesses, long since closed. This part of Castle Street has seen much new residential development. In 1927 Roland Dawkins was named in Kelly's Directory as proprietor of The Castle Motor Garage, telephone 551. For many years they traded from 155, 157, 159 Castle Street, but by 1950 they were no longer listed in the Directory.

An early photograph of the Rising Sun in Castle Street. It has been sad to see the decline and fall of the Rising Sun, especially when Salisbury seems to foster a growing number of new inns and alehouses. During the 1970s, Gary Nunn, 'folk singer and entertainer extraordinaire' ran a popular folk club in the bar, where by request he would sing *The Herring is the King of the Sea,* amongst other well-known numbers. The pub had a riverside garden (with a huge cedar of Lebanon tree) that subsequently became a car park. For a while the building functioned as a nightclub, following extensive refurbishment, but even 'Sunny's' was to hear time being called. This part of Castle Street is also now in residential use. Archers Court was developed by Mccarthy & Stone in 2002.

Whitfield Cosser, photographer of Castle Street, took this 1905 view of the thoroughfare looking towards Salisbury. It is in many ways a gem of a photograph showing a busy street with people gathered about and carriers going about their business. Much of the view has changed with the demolition of both the Rising Sun Inn on the right and Milford House on the left. The latter, covered with ivy in this view, was the home of Richard Dear, a wine and spirit merchant. Whitfield Cosser might well have visited the Rising Sun, as he established his studio at 80 Castle Street at about the time of this photograph.

This part of Nelson Road has changed very little through the ages, at least as far as external appearances go. In the early years of the twentieth century Roland Chapman set up his post office and shop on this corner and it continued to serve the community for three generations before closing in the eighties. The end of the road became a cul-de-sac when the roundabout and ring road were built in the late 1960s.

At the end of Nelson Road, a tollgate and bridge were established by Thomas Scammel in 1899. The bridge created an opportunity to cross the Avon without having to divert to the next bridge either up or down the river. On 22 July 1931 the last toll was paid, the bridge and gate having been sold to the Salisbury Corporation. This scene from 1907 shows few changes today although the gatekeeper's shed, entrance piers and gates have now gone. It is worth recording that the bridge underwent some restoration and maintenance recently, when it was noted by the MP for Salisbury that it was looking dilapidated. The bridge is now more useful to pedestrians and cyclists, as the road is a cul-de-sac, but it does link up with the riverside walks and cycleways.

Castle Road looking towards Victoria Park in around 1910. It is perhaps surprising to see how most of the houses in these views are identical after almost a hundred years. In 1912, George Adey lived at No. 14 while Miss E.B. Farr occupied No. 16. Their houses seem to have gone, presumably demolished to make way for the ring road. On the left-hand side of this road lived George Norton, dairyman; S. Curtis, painter; H.C.B. White, clerk; W.J. Rousell, P.O. clerk; and at No. 70, John Wort, builder. Mr White and his neighbour, S. Biggs, shared the date 1897 on their semi-detached Victorian house. These residents may have enjoyed the recreational facilities offered at nearby Victoria Park. The park was opened to commemorate the Queen's Golden Jubilee in 1887. This was open countryside in 1880, and just a few villas cluttered around the Park Lane area. In 1920, the houses were already reaching away from medieval Salisbury, paradoxically stretching back up the ancient road to Old Sarum, thereby reuniting the two settlements. By the 1960s, much of the land between these two places had been tamed by suburban encroachment.

Bowerhill, just off St Mark's Avenue, was the rather grand home of the Watson family, photographed here in about 1900. From the 1930s it was used as a preparatory school, and once a gale blew the roof off. Like the neighbouring Grange it has now been demolished, Bowerhill disappearing in 1990. Contemporary housing here now at Ventry Close, curiously, features mock timber framing, once also a feature of the grand houses in this area of Salisbury.

This photograph, taken by Norman Lake in the 1960s, captured the commencement of the new city ring road development at the junction of St Mark's Road and Estcourt Road. A terrace of houses disappeared (already begun in this view) to provide space for the large roundabout and then, following the demolition of houses on the left, Churchill Way was built parallel to Estcourt Road leaving the latter a quiet slip road leading to Bourne Hill.

The High School for Girls on London Road also fell victim to the needs of traffic, and was demolished to create space for the St Mark's Roundabout in 1969. It was a richly decorated and substantial building with an attractive gabled roof. Its previous position is now marked by the slip road into Estcourt Road.

Leaving the City of Salisbury in Victorian times by way of Winchester Street would have lead the traveller to London Road (now part of Rampart Road) and the first public house to come into view would have been the London Road Inn, which is depicted in this photograph produced round 1903. The licensee at that time was Charles Bartrum who seems to have managed the inn for just a relatively short time. Having taken over from William Griggs in 1902, he had been replaced by 1906. His successor was Henry Bundy.

Chapter 5

EAST OF THE CITY CENTRE

There remains a public house on the site but presently it is known as the Winchester Gate.

This cathedral view was taken from what is now known as Tollgate Road, seen in the modern photograph. This is the site once occupied by the Greyfriars, who gave their name to the Friary, and the fields here were once known as Bugmore. The city watercourses returned to the Avon here, one having first passed through a watermill. The pile of flints and the roadmaker's shovel are a sign of the developments that were to come, the construction of Southampton Road in 1890. Yet, behind the modern housing can still be seen the line of lime tree pollards leading to St Osmund's Church.

This old view from around 1900 was taken near to the New Inn in Southampton Road. There have been considerable changes here. In the modern photograph, taken by Peter Daniels, we are looking towards the Tollgate Inn and the junction of St Ann Street, St Martin's Church Street and Rampart Road. The New Inn traded from a corner site and occupied several eighteenth and nineteenth-century domestic buildings and a seventeenth-century barn. Just across the road from the inn were the ramparts of the old city wall.

The Sarum Invicta Leather Works in Paynes Hill, photographed by Don Cross in 1965, before its demise. The former factory and warehouse stood rather incongruously, considering the smelly business of leathermaking, next to a handsome Georgian-style house, formerly occupied by peter Daniel's grandparents, just uphill slightly from the old Barnards Cross chequer. A hoist on the third floor of the leatherworks was used for moving heavy materials into and out of the building. Standing on the site of the former Works are now smart new town houses, 55–69 Paynes Hill. Invicta was an old name given to earlier houses which once stood here.